On the Material

On
the
Material

STEPHEN COLLIS

Talonbooks

Talonbooks
Box 2076, Vancouver, British Columbia, Canada V6B 3S3
www.talonbooks.com

Typeset in Meridien and printed and bound in Canada on 30% post-consumer recycled acid-free paper.

First Printing: 2010

The publisher gratefully acknowledges the financial support of the Canada Council for the Arts; the Government of Canada through the Book Publishing Industry Development Program; and the Province of British Columbia through the British Columbia Arts Council and the Book Publishing Tax Credit for our publishing activities.

Library and Archives Canada Cataloguing in Publication

Collis, Stephen, 1965–
  On the material / Stephen Collis.

Poems.
ISBN 978-0-88922-632-6

  I. Title.

PS8555.O4938O6 2010   C811'.54   C2009-906973-3

for Cathy, Hannah & Sophie

CONTENTS

4 x 4

I Fought the Lyric and the Lyric Won

Gail's Books

4 x 4

The only form of resistance is to move.
—David Harvey

LET ME SPEAK CLEARLY

We were in the last days of the
Poem   sun glinting off countless new and identical
Condo towers   hand around the warmth of
Gourmet coffee   car idling at the curb

We were wondering what could still be said
About the reality of cities   building façade
And street   murmuring walls   and oppressive corners
And lost within the petrified world   some lone figures

In perpetual motion   or take these brashly made-up dolls
Carcasses   loose heads and body parts
The extinct architectures of a public's window sphere
Restoration World   Crate and Barrel   John Fluevog

Sign outside a glittering bank tower
Jump you fuckers
Molten money running in the gutters
Some other clampdown   we'd rather not work for

But probably will   austere dreams of outdated ecologies
Give me needy storms of action
That far science takes us
Something outside the free speech zone   the safe assembly area

We were anxious about the market of everything
About the sound of our voices in the cavernous dome
The birds and trees we'd make note of
Our normally articulate mouths splayed across the big screen

This was just a few days ago
The wind across the pages of our pre-digital expressions
A tomahawk   missiled to our chests   plane wing
Dinner fork   something dead but still dominant

We were killing them softly   the planet sighed
None of this and all of this found its way
Into the poem   we were people poking
Around the wreckage   no one had read the reports   no one replied

1

Rush out into space perhaps
It's tomorrow gleaming carbon fuel
Streams rockets to remember this *was*
What the future looked like Walt

Now we're gulping down deserts
Georgia O'Keeffe bones gleaming your
Skin barked beautiful tree lean
Out over gulfs of exasperated oil

Or perhaps it wasn't that at all
Force in a landscape converting currencies
Predict storms taking digital numbers
Off screens and scattering them on the wind

Recursive like tree rings like quatrains
Before the ride's darkness is over
In a blink *au revoir* mysterious presence
You were commerce before the first gasp

2

Got in a truck and
Drove it so like
Hemi or wheel spin
Clunk clutch over

Log rumble hump
To river bed bounce
I can rev but
What solution to

Chance like bigger ones
Chunk chunking a
Donkey in those woods
They once hauled ass

So prescient in their
Destructions their
Mud-flecked muscle
To unwind a little grouse

3

Goodbye Ruby Super Tuesday
The elect have left
For another shining city
Dubai indoor skiing

Or a life in one container
Or another much the same
So grief gathers Volvos
On indestructible vacant lots

And cities go green
From new ethics or old rot
(still to be determined)
The chatter of light rail

Over sleeping bags and shopping carts
The question remains when
Front-runners change with every new day
Who could hang a vote on you?

4

Roads fold and underwrite
Fabled parks and
Mountain enclosures
Sure we found our way

Into Robert Frost's cabin
Burnt some furniture and
Puked on his rug
But it doesn't necessarily

Say anything about poetry
How pines grow beetleless
In deserts where rain
Is only an imagined occurrence

Picked apples   stopped by
Woods   throw-away disneyfied
Vacances   Now it's just
News trying to stay news

5

Yet recall the affinities of class
Have a great tree to branch
Out a feebler life which
Branches the surface beautiful

Every crop is   hunger
Every computer an extension of   "me"
Finding ways depends upon
Deeper swarm theories

Like look at this tree ablaze
Its incineration "self" organized
Or the rhythmic applause
Of a crowd   teams of robots

And every caribou knew
When it was time to run
Some relation other
Than economic between them

6

Here's our parachute
Wonderful as vertigo
Here's a world crisis
We can jump off into

Backyard pool under
Helicopter surveillance and
Shortwave spot-lit
Whispered communiqués

Where language recants
We travel towards each other
The continents touch
Or the south slips off the radar

As the planes continue east
Where the oil is where
In the rubble of war we
Find a tattered Rabelais

7

Here is a claw I
Took from a crab and now
Pretend to pinch at people with
Allegorical delight

Here all the movies are
Repentant rather than celebratory
The neoliberal screen shivers light
Spills onto faces poor with soda-frothed lips

Here the market's mechanisms
Just aren't working anymore
Upsetting applecarts and
Running off with spoons

Here we become vehicular like
A turnpike off-ramp roadside truckstop
Phone booth pulse pulse rickety
Shit-shop where hubcaps collect the sun

8

Though not a word is said about
The French Revolution
The eve of vagrants in
The houseless woods

I shall concentrate instead
On words which tend to occlude
I have myself a region worth
Neglect and ceaseless governance

As 1793 fades   we begin
A process no passage conveys
The material needs of
Minds sounding exhortations

Ruin transformed into *my* italics
Hope's my elision's brilliant apogee
Your throng the ode's well
No immediacies visionary gleam

9

It's not that I advocate errantry
It's that movement says rive
Says write a tree out of place   sea
For a sense of pasture

It's free radicals
Stone to porch presence
Trade that lumbers into the
Planks of houses no one affords

It's equity sails ships
Plywood plies seas and
Breathes on the backs of
Mountains shagged

It's penultimates or bombs
A forest fire with water or beetles
It's democratic to desist
Governing your where   perhaps your when

10

Here we're allowed
To rake a tin cup across
Our invisible bars
Making racket of no difference

Here I have a spontaneous affinity
Your skylark is   my skylark
Your rudimentary form
Is my rudimentary form

Western Canadian Place and
Avenues of Americas
The blood drains towards the border
But the oil is pumped to the head

I'm trying to get even more famous
Jabberwocky   spit a skeleton out
And call it the next big thing
That's how I roll   *documenta   bienniale*

11   *for Jeff Derksen*

I'm in Calgary so I pretend
To be American
Wrecked cars and buried treasure
Oil sands the size of four Vancouver Islands

Parataxis is as simple as
McDonald's / Subway / Mac's
What narratives do we need
If all we are doing is eating?

Viscous deposits like a toothpaste tube
Of money squeezed under the muskeg
Brobdingnagian technologies flexing
Fools willing to fund prophets like lucre

Like filthy rivers reward   (this is
Where we walked)   our cognitive map
Spread out on the dash as we
Get lost in these new and enormous realities

12

We "feel free" because we lack
The gears to shift down to
The articulation of our unfreedom
As we ride across our fraudulent estates

But it is in your grove I would walk
Like a sequitur seeking a non
Denatured poem or fake math
History so fanged   begins to bite back

But   arrested auditor of books   we have
A mere toehold in life   words which are really
Clouds   forced to behave mimetically
Naming Poe is the same as naming a tree

I think the longest hour of all is when
The trucks have gone   little scholars
I think utopia is when   without solution
We invent a new space out of the coordinates of the old

13   *after Rilke*

Archaic torso of   Toronto
Shattered pavement on Bloor and
Bathurst   hurt feet sidewalk
Scar of tramcar   track

These brick facades are so
Old and full of rentable
Emotion   these bay windows
So cluttered with nonsense goods

People clutch pillows in the
Stink of the Greyhound station
Here we are all racially profiled
Here we are taser armed   ready   routine

Even communicative   everything mobile
Nothing but   net   there's nowhere
We're not seen here   cameras   cones
Of light   you must change your   ideology

14

Looking out the window I will
SUV all over this   tarmac world
Fog lights on   suburban gladiator grill
Crunch of rock under tire

Don't talk about it and it will
Go away like changing *un*employment
Insurance into *em*ployment insurance
Buffalo bubble man filling the

Intersection with airy spheres
Was the richest   now the poorest
Hotel Europa nowhere near namesake
Junta seizes   high-energy biscuits

We are mass and how can you avoid that
Beehive   hold a vote on thinnest limbs
The hive that art is   the tree in the dark
Of the Knox   moving flesh and Rothko light

15

There's something in this figure
Squares of cities   tires on a truck
The great abandoned broken projects
Ruins of the mind   they are what compel

What lead to   new beginnings
What's in the old   doctor of storms
Bring me things from farthest places
Coffee beans   microchips   biomedical dollars

I cannot capture open heart but maybe
Dream its artisans   their localities
I pass by on my way to else
Perhaps a city block   perhaps a glen

Then it is indeed a world upside down
Write it   material being
Perhaps the weather has been good to us
Though we've never seen the winter

16

Here isn't but here is
Becoming moreso   four-sided
Object   I could stack you into
Structure or four on the floor

Like three on the tree
Rip across texture of
The city announced by
Corporate logos

Auto body politic or comfy
New slave quarters   you choose your
Illusion I'll choose mine   the erasure of
Signs marking logo ghosts

Here it's just that easy but it
Costs the most   tin cup of complaint
Your skylark   your revving fire
Here   I whisper   *you take the wheel*

17

So I find another line
Of work   perhaps it's
Railroads or pilot boats
Perhaps it's the electric wires

Going sizzle over suburban head
(Couldn't we have a say in
Our own being cooked?) I
Nudge the pen closer to the sleepy

Politicos saying write saying trees
Canopy our love for one another
This square block of text
Tells you I'm here bub but

Perhaps it's difficult to hear
That men and women die miserably
Every day for lack of what is
Found branching left and right

18

Or not left and not right just
Everybody's autonomy though
The paradox of autonomy is
It doesn't drive beyond itself

Rental vans and borderless workers
Rushing them into new engagements
And new risks like "experimental" or
"Linguistically innovative" or

"Indeterminate"   valuable as such
But absent the imaginative work of
The social forces and struggles that
Animate poetic legislators averse

To a generation happy to be
Turning in a circle that won't
Let us point in any particular direction
(Like "formalism" or "engagement")

19

Let's forget the proprietors of
Literary movements   goulash in the pan
Or a sense of the world as
A drawer of broken things

Amongst which a note bearing the words
"Social life" is found
(this is the archive, stupid) Michelet breathing
In the dust of the trees and the workers who made

The paper   authors auguries and unconsidered
Myriads of spiders banding together to spin webs
Hunt prey and even care for one another's
Offspring (*salut*   my little children)

An ecological niche not available
To solitary individuals and free of
Top-down hierarchies   Vichy hostesses   soup
Tureens   or as Derrida indicated   *house arrest*

In the wake of change   chains
Men made decoy obedience
Difficult to discriminate
A period of throws   the very language of deceit

We were in a novel   tennis court oaf
The profane skies did complement the clowns
And polite citizens sentenced themselves
Shackled by arbitrary restraints

Did somebody say pastiche?
The bare parts of a great series   Mind forged mandibles
In some future period (Noble Apostrophe)
The language of Romance   not the cold formality of Statutes

I'll no longer pursue the gaudy ghost
Or (to borrow the language of the world)
Went in the middle of the night and broke the padlocks
Threw open the gates   in the wake of chains   change

21

Limits   are what we are combined of
But where there is a boundary
There is also a   beyondery
Like *I-fought-the-lyric-and-the-lyric-won*

It's a pulp and paper planet   beetles
Invading ponderosa lodgepole scots and
Bristlecone   21.5 billion
Board feet (2005)   stumping for stumpage fees

Boring through bark and producing pheromones
Mass attacks carrying blue stain fungi
Trees phloem layer overwhelmed trees
Starve reddening needles entire groves   O

Ikea   this furniture is fine but what
Are these strange names and relentless allen keys
For?   sibling tree economies
All capitalizing on lumbering   snoozing insect wars

Wood   I compose sleep near
Verse saying come astrologers
Envision the clocks   listen to dreams
Imports blown upon trade winds

Soft mist blooms noir nature
Toil in blue-lamped windows
Plumes of carbon mount the firmament
Verse's pale encampment illumed

Shivering spring winter autumn
When our veranda shivers monotonous snows
We foment party politics   *et voilà*
Pour batter down neat-freaks' palaces

Their gardens built of innocent words
Their boughs knocking at window's pain
With burning thoughts mute temptation
My pensioner's brilliant unity almost here

23

I want trees   a place to plant them
A means of being okay
And you too a bough of your own
To occupy above the flood

'Til the helicopters get here
(If they get here)
Wildfires surrounding the suburbs
A tsunami on some vacationing shore

It's the tanks you keep in your pockets
Of resistance   a barrel of oil burnt
It comes of thirst and engines
Besieging the remaining television stations

Perhaps there's a narrative thread
Perhaps something you still need
Can be found hanging from these boughs
Or trailing along behind in the current

24

In a world of short attention spans
Poems proliferate
Along a continuum of lonely utterances
Stopped just inside electronic mouths

Not Kant unravelling reason's mechanics
But Rumsfeld insisting insurgents
No longer be called "insurgents"
The word giving greater legitimacy

Than they "deserve"   no corpus
Beyond sound-bit ears
The thumb coming to rest at the creased
Corner of the page   or upon a keypad button

Its number worn off by critiques of pure unreason
While just out of eyesight
Insurgent beetles find a bit of cone or freedom
Fighters forget—are we for or against "freedom"?

25

The only form of resistance
But it *costs* so much
And those gulls falling from
Trailing contrail spires

Would make a lovely poem
I could travel half a continent
To read it to you
In an air-conditioned room

No man an island but
Archipelagoes have weathered storms
Even when form is no planet's friend
We are lumbering   material

Shackled to peddling pirates
We push up the long hill   gassed
And ontologically uncertain
The lyric stream undermining the langue bank

26

I hang my head in a pictorialist halo
Nothing need be added from the artist's
Inner consciousness   plums or the pose
Of indigents   in vagrant woods

So I'll focus over here for a second
The body's torsion lines its global
Flows and formalist frames
Finger on the pulse of light poured

Having beheld us drowsing in the
Frozen clasp of science I click click you
Into my eye forever new beauty truth of an
Old world study in red the crowd

Overexposed   I point at the street its
Lyric light schooled its cadences
Victorian Victor Hugo's shadow disappearing
Behind a barricade of newly made machines

27

Perhaps it's the century
Blood tearing its bleary eyes
Perhaps it's all this exhausted space
Converted to time's electric calculi

As Frost's lost lectures tell us
It's pretty easy to see I'm an American
Fools foolish enough to confront fools
We'd lose all that when capitalism goes

Notes from nowhere the
Delete the borders movement
The weardown of the material world as
The precariate heads into the long weekend

Perhaps it's that you insist me
My body of global wounds scattered amidst
The wars of greedy men and the *facteur* Cheval
Finding this stanza   a stone in his field

28   *for Colin Browne*

We navigate by trees the
Faultlines in a language of
When and maybe   where
Fertile ravines water drops through

Foraging needles from rivulets downed
A small plane its passengers
Pertinent facts how we all
Came here   ancestored   cold

An unwilling accession from the
Genetic commons   the putrid spoils
Of desert wars and roadside
Bombs improvising metallic blooms

Each tree tells a way home to the
Page   each tree I camp beside in my
Lexicon   its limits and its limbs
Its sprint   at the finish   of its form

29

The poison in my body in the globe
Versus the mindset that thinks
If it can be done   it should be done
Is this poem helping at all?

This computer won't let me spell
Bioserfdom or *biopiracy*
Brick after brick the
Wall of patents   rises before us

To get across as gropes
I touch you   touching poetry
The sleeve of ink
The patter of fingertips pressed

Its lisp to the border patrol
Its workers not working the west
A tree nearby in light bending
Its boughs reaching   just over the wall

30   *after Goethe*

I call him   surface
This sea of error   the very things
Wither   the sad little houses
The fires   hurrying

I want wings   the ground
The eternal beam of every fold
The hilltops flowing into streams
Gashed and savage   like amazed inlets

Daughter languages   otter wolf lynx
Bee honey cattle sheep and
Spoke-wheeled horse languages
Riding out of the Indo-European steppes

Venerable parchment   burnt flax
Of throats the body warms in
The flight from page to page
To the edge of evergreens   on abrupt cliffs

What deals with devils what
Sprang from our texts hungry not
Change to being the change we become
But hungry deals to keep same's reign

An author for your functions
Selected from my Google brethren
My searchable ghosts bearing
Identity into diverging links

So I house two souls in me
And each from each wants separation
With battered organs
Carry me   where a bright life comes

Out of the desert   fire on fire
The swarming west   blackhawks into view
Valkyries   be the change you want changed
Once you have smashed this world to smithereens

32

How do we know it *is* late?
Dark stage   commodity at my elbow
Supposedly connecting everyone everywhere
Its musical sheen   its practiced sleekness

Marvels never cease
Seeming to be marvelous
Acts caught on film
The pummelling of bodies   material

And immaterial   the vacation pay
The flex days   could there be a better
Way of doing business?   air strikes
Not tax hikes   the sad thrill of   loans

The letter carrier knows his dying breeds
Their long-toothed Wednesdays
Their winters   forms
It's too far gone   for it only to be late

33

The fleet drifts in on an angry tidal wave
Cameras at the ready
Dolphins and orca whales preparing their tricks
And a sub testing its missiles in Nanoose Bay

As old lumber peels its hide outside
Ladysmith and Lake Cowichan a
Beaver buzzing Victoria's inner harbour
My inner-ear telling me   I'm off balance

Or kilter   sighting along old log booms my
Father's eyes looking into the water of his
Childhood as pilots steer history between
Nations of rocky debt and sovereign precarity

After all   we made money out of matter here
Now condos shield us from the computer hum
Of on-line trading   and wars flash on flat screens
As 4x4s cool and ping   mud covered in double garages

34   *for Roger Farr*

What an effective device we have here
Opposable thumbs and an upright gait
Mind with a tool or weapon inside
Pictured half-cocked trigger twitched

What verbal equipment for storied storms
Myths we have lived by
Will to move earth and water works
I am poetry   hear me mingle

What a get-up the finery of beliefs
Versions of viability and the
Division of spoils   a tree cut down
Becomes a little wooden idol or

Cellular phone   then old log booms
And elections for the parliament of tricks
A few beetles   left alone throwing dice
On the vast salt deserts of the Americas

35

There are limits   the intentions
Of the boundless   manifest in the agony
Of boundaries   the sticks in the mud
Of the harbour   or all my father's years

A war of planes in the air above his head
As pilots steer history between the
Charybdis of dementia and the Scylla of
Million-dollar views   whose woods we

Stop by   on our way south
And he gives his artist's bells a shake
Or points at tiny black and white
Photographs saying perhaps I was   perhaps

I went   and we become the nameless agency
Of movements unimagined generations project
Wondering who will see us stopping here and
Who shall speak of us when we are gone

36   *for Rita Wong*

The best lines of this generation are quotations
Buy Rita Wong's *Forage* and read it
Via a biochemical process called "cognition"
While an untold fund of toxins pulses

Throughout my various bodily systems
The fruit on the table too plump and bright
My father's eyes as pilots steer
History between the transgenic trees

And this luxury condo where we sort
Old photographs under designer lighting
Dear bloated monstrosity   can we recycle
Our pasts or make these images trees again?

Here we might ask whether our arrangement as
Autonomous members of a group is more like
Smarties in a box or the heap of computer
Circuit boards cascading from the cover of this book

37

The titles only exist in some
Imaginary appendix or table of
Contents   look under trouble
Shoot   tailgate   loveseat

I read others' books I wish I'd written
Kevin Davies standing in *my* graveyard
The mangled fabric of fences
A dirt road   you could almost drive down

You probably don't remember this
But we were *all there*
Expressing ourselves on the expressway
And going on and off road   signifying like crazy

We're all shot now   and police muffle
Our android names in electric sleep
Another fourth of the month picked off its balcony
Now keep moving, this comma is here for you

38   *for Yvette Poorter*

Each tree standing alone in its stillness
This neck of the woods the
Mantle of the poor or given global
Swarming no mantle for these misfortunes

News from the avant-garde dailies
Speech and I are just friends
Electricity passes through us to an island
Our water comes through fifty kilometres of pipe

Space inhabits and   inhibits
I feed the neighbour's cat   clean up
After the raccoons   it's new normalism
For the lords of the water mountains

Is disjunctive irony all we can expect
From poets now   no question mark there
This is history in a virtual age
Treeless I ask   who ate the blackberries?

39

I remember you from the blackout
The fleet before the tidal wave
Your dolphins strapped to bombs
All the tuna   in a sea of cans

Perhaps the streets were deserted
The monuments bent to brush their shoes
As an ambulance spelt itself backwards
It's a time-eat-space sort of world

Thunder came to kill our industries
Mythic birds   their liquid crystal eyes
Making all the money of trees liquid
Lazy beetle days   in the acidic soil

Perhaps we came by all this naturally
A vent in the earth   in the "globe"
My father's eyes the sightlines of trees
Disappearing   each tree   is introspection

40

The dreams were   unremarkable
Failed chanteuse in the hotel lobby
Sex and money linked in men's brains
A reduction on footprints   offensive zones

Or complete absence of Starbucks
I want to speak to you about your
Open vowels   *stone plash boat earth*
Waver purl close hove

Blood disk or horizon flame
Cloud hanging over concrete viaducts
Cold-cocked in the urban archive by
Walter Benjamin's free hand

Perhaps you are where   perhaps
You are when   it's neither April
Ghosts nor April galleons   but
Defunct music burns on the water all day

41

Apropos of appropriation
I take a lyric from your limit
Please excuse the plums from your fridge
They were so old I had to throw them out

Vis-à-vis Joshua Clover
Is it history or capitalism that enters
That phone booth   or just Batman and Robin
Fluttering through centuries of cartoon accumulation

It's thus that immediacies visionary gleam
Reams of unwrit paper   porch junk   a pack
Of Camel cigarettes   (by Benjamin's other hand)
The free fountains of Portland forever flowing

Some freighter stopped by urban docks
To watch containers fill up with products
Was I born in a half-savage country   out of date?
Allow me my accelerated grimace   my obstinate isles

42   *after Donato Mancini*

Roadtrip tripwire ire irenic
Nicotine inedible bleach each
Ache cheaper aperture tureen
Re-enter entertains insurance ancestor

Storehouse houseboat boater terrace
Race acentric tricolor oloroso
Rosolio lioness essentials also
Soba bamboo boony-bash Basho

Ashore Oregon gongoozler Lerner
Nerve verver vervain vainglory
Lory ryokan Okanagan Gandhi
Dhikr Kropotkin kingfisher sherpa

Pacific fiction ionizer zeroth
Otherwise wiseacre acreage agenda
Gendarme armed media dialectic
Ticklish Ishmael maelstrom Strombopolous

43   *for Andrea Actis*

Perhaps it's a country you remember
Its exhaustion and its fish grottos
The time it takes to bait its bears
Space you crossed   escaping bylaws

North of attention but south of
Their tents on the hills of incremental invasion
No other relation than economic between us
Mi casa   su casa   mon payee

I love a wall   doesn't build us
This world gone 4x4ing over wrack and
Ruin   no barricades built of asphalt
Bio born to break or better   bend

Perhaps it's furtive human help
A hand held out to cavernous combs
The honey in that land we milked
Hoping for the opening of other eyes

44   *for Jordan Scott*

Then rain comes to draw the city's lines
Telephones face books that breathe
Autre words a nest in the sentence
Trees cats and urban cyclists reform

Umbrella poetics their viva thirsts
Catastrophes speaking Germanic strophes
Dumb music of spheres and global
Gluttony outside the closed Lebanese restaurant

We coo tongues riff tonsil textures a
Yawp for bardic hopes maps of
City after city turned on topography's
Lathe or wave after wave of merging tropes

Then I saw the word   Paris
The street cobble jolt jolt jolt jolt of
Spine after spine of books the forgotten
Art of building stone walls to better   breathe

THE ARK OF RESISTANCE

But maybe we could still winch this rig
Out of the ditch   a bottle-rocket beginning
Molotov cocktail party   some urban druids
Chanting round stone dolmen dumpsters

Someone said surrealism   but it was
Space not clocks they were melting
The asphalt turning to oil   the silver planes
No one   not even armies   could afford to fly

This was the desert of desires after all   commodity
Frozen in the process of feeling itself up
Just managing to whisper   *oil can … oil can*
Through clenched tin lips

And then looking up at the empty sky
Someone yells   *arc of resistance*
Rainbow or triumphal promenade of cloud form
Rain storm coming to quench all this killing

But what I heard was   *ark of resistance*
And there it was   black hull   and red sail
Crewed by pre-emptive Parisians in red liberty caps
Kid with pistols   woman's bare breast   flag

And so we gave up   vehicle for vessel   false freedoms
Audi allroad m-class range rover sport
Cayenne turbo steptronic jeep cj 4runner
Explorer expedition land cruiser pathfinder ram

Hummer hummer hummer hummer
F-150 250 350 superduty durango hemi
Tacoma tundra tucson sierra savannah denali acadia
Escape edge ram ram ram ram   liberty

And then we slipped aboard the ship   and past the pier
And then I saw my comrades course before the mast
And then the wind came   red sail   even keel
And then I saw horizons future-lit burst bright beyond the frame

I Fought the Lyric and the Lyric Won

THE END OF FLIGHT

What cold fatigue brings this
Tree's bough to the ground
Handful of nails out of
My pocket last light from
The sky as I turn
Towards the house the dead
Eagle fresh in memory in
The soil I just buried
It in head gone (crows)
It fell from the tree
Where it had been hung
Up a few days growing
In smell and losing feathers

This means good luck I
Tell the hedge I toss
The left over nails into
This means I ought to
Build more complex structures just
A play house today for
Two daughters running up shout
This means build I think
The architectures of dream the
Streaming columns rooms of gold
With poetry walls all jade
And gleaming and dark with
Night and wanting the firey
Posts shining lintel and above

This I'll hang a flaming
Bird and its eternal flight
Will take whatever I have
Built with it into the
Sky behind the sky feathers
Falling spiral through the boughs

I'm not quite sure why
The bottom of my foot
Hurts I'm not quite sure
Where I am when I
Say *here I am* clover
Overtaking the back yard a
Faint desire to eat fresh
Berries to wing my way
Towards some other undreamt work
Weather eye open hammer and
Some boards busy in my
Father's chest a canoe in
The clouds maybe I reach
Home after many years it
Is unbuilt in memory and
For sale all this time

ARISTAEUS MOURNING
THE LOSS OF HIS BEES   *for Sharon Thesen*

Were the bees …
… or where the hive?
the drive home
to the honey of place
no trace
to return to die singly
far from home the
buzz buzz of cell
phones form the
absence the empty hives
along this untravelled apian
way calling *have you*
seen him small and
mottled like a cinder he
died alone though many
shared a similar fate
stung and silvered at
their electric cars

Out over the water a
cell phone's silver
wings beat faster than
the eye can see the swarm
turns in the arc of air
ruptured by container ships
coursing east / west
each small cell its
capital sweet to gather
to keep to
lose your way home
to the hive
where there are no bees but
a silver cell
phone sits humming (on
vibrate) in blue light
encased in grey
papers coiled

Bees are interrupted
transmissions dropped
calls to the colony
like did you hear me
when I said *we*
are in a good deal of
trouble (globally) and the
night set the sea above
mountains blue with
flowered fields and
your cell was the only
light left to light the
way back out of
whatever it was we
were left with
shuttling commodities

Whir the bees or the
pollen fallen the
honey pours from the
mouths of dead poets
there are cells in every city
(terror stricken)
the locus is links
chains of communication
the bees have gone
inactive as the
fields have turned
electric the pulses
beat against the heads of
poppies and puppet
regimes in fields of
force I meet a bee
exhausted and far
from its hive
weak it gasps
hold my calls

I call but the bees I
know aren't there their
accounts emptied
small hollow bodies
found far from their
hives along highways
containers pass
on the backs of trucks
sick with chemical
and bacteria born
a single hole
in each tiny head
execution style their
cell phones checked for
any final calls I
get home just after
the truck leaves too
late our home is
no longer ours a cipher of
no place or
my bees have left me
with a bitter pill to swallow

I have seen them
swarm or singly
falter along a dusty
window ledge
alone is nothing
the bee buzz keeps
coming my solitude
is bundled and has
a camera built into it
keeping you connected
means receive this alone
unable to raise
a host of foragers
they die somewhere
flying all night and
dropping one by one
as exhausted pellets
upon petals that
closed with the dew

But the bees are
not math a memory
no photograph
the calipers used to
remove the corpse or
set the chip in place
are covered with honey
a meadow remains
a bee sting on the
bride's foot a river
with a severed head
still talking into its
orphic cell floating
down to the sea
singing its plaintive
ring tone to which
no bees respond

THE HISTORY OF PLASTIC

Simple molecular configurations
of carbon and hydrogen atoms
linked together to form chains
(all we have to lose are our chains)
mixing tarry carbolic acid
phenol with formaldehyde
in Yonkers Leo Baekeland
et voilà—a green sea turtle
in Hawaii dead with a pocket comb
a foot of nylon rope and
a toy truck wheel lodged in its gut

Fish may not know they are in water
what alien realm awaits us
Great Pacific Garbage Patch
unable to breathe and cancer
coating our colons
cracking long hydrogen chains
of crude petroleum into smaller molecules
mixing fractionates
add chlorine for PVC
blow in gas linking bubbles
for polystyrene
defining modernity
in pure clear flexibility
a torrent of products into the
widening gyre

We were bones in our shapes
the nylon sheath of
surface pulled taught over structure
unseen but revealing its presence
through its limitless exchange of
one function for another

this happy meal toy giblet

this fine fibre optic filament

this now unneeded breast implant

this tire between you and the
road's sudden commercial curve

Is language
plastic
the body the mind
plastic?
The idea of
malleability before
material itself became
malleable
formed for every toxic thought
we wanted a soft world
for it to conform to the hand
as if exchangeable
reproducible
cheap and throwaway
not thinking of decay
of a throwaway world
shaped to our hands
hurling everything
its soft objectivity and
currency over the walls of
our mortal enclosures

Does any of this stuff ever
go away?

Creaks under its own
weight

Am I angry
at products or production?

Stand by a polymer sea amidst
bladder wrack and cockle shell
micro waved inside a
nylon windbreaker
looking at countless nurdles
we thought just colourful sand

Is making itself
the problem?

How did we go from
meeting our needs to
excess and waste?

History of plastic
History of capitalism

Can we say that word?
Opaque everything or
impotent opiate
Dear common I tell you
commodity makes us
cancer when we think
constant growth is
the only answer

Only disease has this
impulsion

Doctor can you cure us?

Yes but we'll have to
cut your economy out

So that was it

A bona fide bona fide

Flame on the canvas where
paint once went

An ugly bit of business
this stock and that

Then we had to *eat*
our children

Rock 'Em Sock 'Em Robots
by Marx toys (acquired by
Tyco   acquired by Mattel)

Is this my pile of crap
or yours
swift movement of
puttied time?

Just listen to the
poets
their hands and
halves of shells

I think this red cup
has made me sick

It's melting on the stove now
while my lungs fill
with the fumes

Even the makers of latex
must sometimes softly
love the world

SELF-PORTRAIT IN A CORVETTE'S MIRROR

Though it's not *my* car
Just passing on the street and
Bent to gawk as the *imago* swerves
Away easily   longing to be free

But locked at the curb it must stay
Parked it must move into paranoiac
Knowledge the function of the eye
Illuminated headlamps englobed in delicate

Meshes of the afternoon as it sheds reflection
Which makes the invisible hand loom large
Over the stick still stuck in motor
Capacity longing to take this performance onto

The rear-view mirror stage all veiled faces
Of owners peaking at oil's eclipse
The window and the trees merging
In one neutral band whose properties

In the silver blur recede into once common
Curving road that   "little reality"
Of the material   its side-impact beams high
Beams high performance of the

Formative self growing wings and
Taking up arms against the illusion of autonomy
Or auto-erogeny   alive with filiations
You realize the reflection in the mirror isn't yours

It's inner arena   and enclosure
Outdone by a   chimpanzee
Even elephants   it seems   recognize
Themselves in silvered glass

So someday try to do as many
Things as possible   still yourself
Performative precocity   the unwinding gearbox
This knowledge of servitude love alone must undo

POEM BEGINNING WITH THE TITLE OF
A CY TWOMBLY PAINTING

Fifty Days at Iliam writing
A small dictionary of debts
Recollecting recompense the structural epic
How we any of us
Depopulate scorn throwing contingency up
On the wounds ethics wears
Or take from a poem
Small candle window worn to
Speak into tongues most fervent
Wry whisper or voices valence

Look—it shook secrets from
Our agents who wore mirth
Like a salient whim or
Chipped sugar onto larks' backs
To swoop from romantic piers
And stupid like we weren't
Ninjas swooping into politics pretending
Farce and forced open our
Ocular throats to bleat against
Gain and murder's plunder gore

Or like this painting where
Each brush stroke is borrowed
From another or tightly coiled
In canvas the culture chirps
In another tree language is

Links everything stolen is free
To form affinity frames light
And pure colourists divine ardour
As a way of being
Oneself in another's delicate skin

This is to be reiteration
Echo quote figure trope troubled
Lyric can you hear me
Now pointillism is my point
To make a mend in
Rent fabrics torn of voice
Scattered and weathered versions thereof
Every poem written as "after"
Subsumed but not bearing debts
Laughter as origin propertyless press

Thus like a fire that
Consumes all before it an
Eagle drops skies scars and
Pallas fierce drives where thickest
Making war or poems without
Fame fled to paint rages
As ages hence we are
Still standing a precipice treed
To overlook our angers destructions
Or boil our debts' oil

Gail's Books

There's still no truth in making sense
—Michael Palmer

An August day garden sun her flower print dress it is our parents 50th wedding anniversary and days later we learn she has cancer and I recall that dress her smile and the sun. On December 19, 2002, my sister Gail dies. Days before enduring her final lucid moments trying to talk and something in her tongue seems gone and as a kind of resignation the only word that comes out again and again is "okay" "okay."

One thing we shared was a love of books and learning. Hers: poetry, psychology, spirituality. Mine: poetry, philosophy, history. Poetry was the hinge, the place our worlds swung one into another's.

On January 19, 2003, one month after the day she died her house burned in an accidental fire. Her study and books destroyed the firemen having cast the burning volumes through broken windows into a yard of rain and darkness. Many land in a small fish pond where I find them blackened soaked and crumbling the next morning. Only one book is recoverable. The fire has taken everything else—anything she had written her books personal effects clothes—any material reminder.

There are other books that were hers and which I took in the month between her death and the fire or which I had as gifts or loans over the years books that remained "hers" indelibly marked no matter how long they had occupied my shelves the hinge between us a book's spreading binding gutter and spine. Kathleen Raine's *Selected Poems* with four purple flags protruding sideways from passages and poems she marked to return to quote or recall. Rilke's *Book of Hours*, a favourite of hers: she bought me a copy too and now I have both hers and mine. Novalis's *Philosophical Writings* and Peter Ackroyd's *Blake* biography with the poet's "Good and Evil Angels" on its cover: tilting its glossy surface in the right light I can make out the impression of a telephone number pressed into the soft cover—a North Vancouver number she no doubt took down using the book as a writing surface her hand has engraved it exactly between the two figures, on the evil angel's outstretched arm and down across the flames sea sky and earth. There are many more—anthroposophical books I have never really read but which seem to embody some outsideness to time that was hers and remains in their covers and inscriptions the material presence upon my shelves of something she called "spirit" but which I appreciated more through her very material and now missing presence.

I hold what she held touching hinges. There is nowhere else she is. The door creeks open to oblivion—hence voices. I try to look where her eyes looked reading reunion. The flag flutters the eye open and closed. August print dresses. May she is born. December she dies and begins again. This was her belief and I can only hold it in my hands and watch the words play across in imperfect print.

RAIN

This slip marks the moment of your absence
books you have left shuttered gifts
glyph or glimpse of reading rent
margins I want marked meander
feeling evening roses sound fear holds chaos against cold

It is questions I would pour into deserts
swamping silence

Go back again
to the time of recollecting
who speaks hears
fragile forests holds
metallic dreaming

If we are any
antinomies affirmations
not holding is an orbit
round the emptiness where
you read aloud to me

Writing to ward off
with words going
into governance to unlock
laws shout out of disasters
We are here We are here

This failing inscribes
on sheer volatility
volumes I cannot read
no matter it was you leaving them
ephemeral rain falling out of rain

These are your
Selected Poems now I
cannot choose otherwise

You are on the edge of
rain the shimmer of
fire forms a screen

Oracles wind Medea
not return murmur
to sorrow go   to nest

I shiver the moment self
incarnates the Pythoness
moves towards origin

Because a tear is an
intellectual thing
this rainfall will
cloud vision towards
deeper thinking where
you keep sleep
in a box and your
voice amongst reeds
will be the presence of
pomegranate seeds
sparkling red multitude
silent and awaiting the
decay of December and
rebirth of May

POLLEN

1.

Think of the dead

The misapplications of the word "liberty"

This common
mixture of failure and thought

Worlds touch at points of
penetration

A flutter of seeds
unseen

So an imaginary how easy
to make a universe fray

Of the concentricity of the word
other
opening its ducts

2.

Homemade beeswax
candles all hanging like
frozen brown rain from
lines strung across the kitchen

What doesn't cause cancer?

Sitting too close to the TV
resin of canoes
cell phones
smoking
red meat

Free markets
unlimited growth
unsustainable monoculture

3.

Each being a society
object the centre of paradise

Fetishes—stars—animals
heroes—divinities—idols

The spurned gem of fair
commerce

This unification is a
free alliance of

The beautiful appears
so much at rest

4.

Each has its claim on every
so things are what are
found between

The sticky gauze of life or

Membranes windows the gummy
surface of the eye

Penetralia travelling on
a bee's bushy leg

5.

Consider the smallest

A caption under a crack

This thistle bodice broach

Caprice of a single strand of hair

A broom bush

Matter

6.

The art of writing books
breaking branches
still if only some grow

Cut or graft a grain of
another authenticity

The character is dithyrambic
constantly poured
into new vessels
it exists only
for autonomous lovers of rain

7.

Philosophy, a caress
countless eclectics now emerge

Poetry dissolves being singular

Each body a problem
thrust towards ourselves

A common movement
towards beloved worlds

8.

We are still living on
the fruit of
better times
Now cut that out

The result can be
a riven stone
a hole for gunpowder
a statue etc.

Out amongst magistrates
flowers gather in a gully

9.

Thinking truly communally
only what is incomplete
can be comprehended

(this means used)

Everything must become food
everything seed

10.

I come back to you
noble Kepler

The centre is perpetual autonomy
curves out to cleave the dark

This is the medical view
of the French Revolution

The plan of their cure
the most accurate image of the future

Solid bodies are necessary for this
in the bleak houses of abstract deists

11.

How few to form a possible history?

I made them out of clay
and unalienated labour

This wing I found
without any bird

Movements of your hands
in front of the
flood of speech
okay okay

This influence of others
you speak of is the purpose

12.

Frisked by ontology
while crossing the border
into the state of nature

She it is
disappearing in the trees
while I try to recollect
the true music of her voice

And the dithyramb
which is the embrace

13.

Your wonder is many
I am one beginning
a bee seems leaningly
a slope into sound

Hum of the shell of you
remains in my ear
a seed of thought
planted to grow gardens

14.

In the hymn I have
to the night left between us
you stand holding a book
no hands can open

I know what's written there:
everything we've yet to say
everything not ourselves
that is ourselves

Stretching beyond us
to touch us

15.

Half in love with ending
Rilke and his rose
Blake and his angels
the bees find a hollow
in the body and build

cell upon cell
their own collective structure
for the sake of
sweet resistance
the mass and *its* beauty
who knows whose home
the body is

I neither come nor go
there is no shuttle
on this loom
no window
looking onto your leaving

No matter how grasped
it falls through the hands

VARIATIONS AND TRANSLATIONS FROM RILKE'S *BOOK OF HOURS*

1. THE NIGHT DIES SICK AND STUNNED, ITS ROOT MIC STILL ON

Book of moods
Music's icon I
Conoclastic steel its
Power is linking its
Rose absolves trees
Here's an hour of
Bees I throw the
Stuffing out of Israel
A spout sky refolding
Wit rye book ink
Siphons wings rays
Home aboard trees
Too sweet to let

2. I'VE SEEN MY LIFE IN WATCHES RINGING

Book of lost circles
Fingered in water I
Teach to rout loss
From the word may
Shot drum beats
This blast sun shot
Eyes live, try twelfth
Movement icicle sound
Shod and bound cry mortal
Flower eyes bees
Winking pour shrouds and
Tears and eyes fill
But don't sow ammo

Welcome morally weak throng
It's an abundance a
Bridge a beginning, too

3. I'LL LEAVE MY VESSELS ANKLE-STUNNED

Book of seeming
Eyes rove Theodorus
Other's being sees sky
Weeps wind an intrusion
Where can I bind them
As in gold fetters
The rays of strife
All beauty, rive, ankled
To rake a levelled wood

Swell, eye, to end times
Mic a bee whispering
"Lover of sheaves," night
And waking feel the stream
Oven on, it's cooking books

A stream wants moss
A rung lower, and tongs

4. WHEN IT'S NORMAL, SO GOES THE WAR

Book of angers the
Phony fronts wars patrol
Fifty nocturne-lit ashtrays hiss
Good commuted to evil after
An ecstatic mystery ache
Fall, love, eternity weeps
While we hum, combing a body-lake

Ten-to-one last sound and cold-wrought
Eye hood-winked
Who Tupperware bickering trends

I could pose guesses too
Eden for levity and a while
Tall sheaves in
Glades west of here
Sense entwining its nonsense

5. DITCH WATER NIXED MY STEAM WATCH

Book of blasted gates
Who isn't comprised of
The office and the home
Who has been owning naught
The bees need their night
Place bets and pool-halls beaming
And who knows—tree
Hum to tree hum—who
Coos to ward off fences
Wing-hymn a strand off the windrow

The Greeks could steal the lumber
From the trees, should those
You fell saunter right back
In the course of editing
How the senses long lines wend
Thrace gone and the wind
Hucks your words over fences
Rife with red sheaves

Though the sense hunches
The lyre strains
Beneath bower and even song
Bee, the sound trying wonder
Bemoans snow, white string
Sharpened till it feels
Taught and you, regal, fall
A tree which teaches true

6. VEIL-LICKED CHURCH OF DIRT, SWEAR AWAY BLUNT GATES

Book of dissolved tears
It's merely resistance
Every wing is closed
Every wing choosing anomie
Hastened to its tone

Wince, eye, shrill coast
Throw stuff, rout gain
Hiss unbearable artfulness
Shake, bee, stall fits
Which throw dresses down

Shard of bee, awake, thin
Ember glow, mine your artfulness
Cloth of the fallen cities
Stone which we effigy
Our nothing which remains
Small

NEVER TO BE POSSIBLE SAID OR SUNG

1.

The house was the house and
not the house

Cloud measured cloud to tell of
time and photography

Beside the house was a barn
that does not exist

I felt the lake's presence without
looking to the left

In the barn   the worn floorboards
began to buckle and lift

While outside people began to gather
and organize themselves into cars

Though I stayed on alone
(as I is want to do in poems)

a hill that does not exist formed suddenly
for my purchase

as in the distance where
a line of cottonwoods ought to be

four dark and whirling tornados appeared

The house flew up   Dorothy
was my grandmother   the hem on

another's dress

Oil an envelope around engine parts

The rain could be coming at any moment.

Furtive, like animals under the eaves   their transformations
their abattoir

I have purchased nothing   but expected every gift

The limits of tell

Do tell

The house sits empty awaiting others

If you were in a barn and if

If was a barn but not a barn a small building beside

Another building covered with a grape vine and

In this smaller building sometimes hummingbirds became
trapped along the window sills

So you had to come cover them with your hands to set them free

If this window this bird a flicker crashed against the pane

If the pane if the flicker a hummingbird blue

If in the barn not a barn the floorboards
not floorboards but concrete

The floorboards began to buckle and lift

If lifting if boards not boards began to lift

Then water was revealed beneath

If water boiling and black began to lift those floorboards
where you know concrete really lies

If this then waking and running to cars

In photography remains yesterday
no neutral no expanse

I shiver at the edge of lettering
letting this go this picture the

Water like wind invisible above invisible
trees

The clouds stretched out of sight out of
the page to tell

Do tell

Of the photographs you named frenzy

And the fire should we mention
should we the fire the

Books curl and clouds unseen

It was night then clouds then blackening curls

I did not look at the lake
on the left a photograph exposed

This dream the lake known but not seen not
there as such as in one

Dream it is such and I alone as I
is want

And watching as storms and isolation leave us
that is this solitary this alone

Tornados emerge and suddenly
high above watching but

There is no looking to the lake at the left

Though the signal is clear and photographs and cancer and
I have only ever been saying goodbye

And the books in flames fell
into the pond in the yard of the house not the house just

Presence and lakes and looking and only one book
survived the fire and flood

To catch hummingbirds hand and an ossuary of sorts

2.

Even her post-it note smoked

In my hands it still smells of smoke

The smoke from the hedges holds

Smoke and I am vapour gone

In the book not the dream smoke

Its cover and pages stiff corners and page ends burnt brown

Damage from smoke and flames on its grey boards smoked and

Water damage at one corner crushed and smoked

But you can still read open up prophecy pretend

Who speaks in the limits is smoke

Whose hand opens the book points threads

Whose sister is the fire forming smoke

Whose ash is now ash's ash

Who walks in that tall flame smoked

A politics rests its hands on its knees

A bird is in one hand it is
a flicker

I open her *Art and Human Consciousness* with care

I open the sail unfurl at night sailing
midst leaves litter

Open vista a hill read the house not
the house of fire or four tornados untrue

And galvanized I gather omens any

Let the bird go it is a political act fleeing commodity

As four tornados as

Swoop and glide

It's a little
Quixote club
All of us trying
Something
Impossible
Factories
Into freshets
Forms
Out of forests
Health for its own sake
The food without the chemical
The home without the hospital
The furnishings without the fortunes
The affinity without the finality

For whom is this *order* so important cosmos and
retail space to let

The earth is shingled outward from within

If we had only managed to interact with our plants

The human measure of the clouds
their distance
their metonymy

As one epoch changes
into what follows

With enough to spend on books and closed borders

The cornices and the capitals
she lives in them
just as she did in
the limbs of her own body

The book open its letters smoking over the white water

Even as we sat quietly
working away in our studies

In the fire
A window opened
In the window
Pages turned
As though a wind
A bird passed
Through my hand
Operas and idleness
Okay it is okay
As though air
I sat by the water
Filled with books
Reading its feathers
Floating in flame

The process which had begun with the
dispute between the Realists and the
Nominalists was now complete

Outwardly the actors held their hands

Like the spiteful toothless mouth of some
horrible cowering ghost

The common people of course did not get to experience
"the time of the Ptolemies"

The tornadoes were pillars of air

These temples built by people calling the world a *cosmos*

Everyone who has *entered* the
interior space of the earth

The house not the house had to dream
people then socialism then the opening
of all throats singing

Up beyond our individual selves

(By Gottfried Richter and translated by Burley Channer and
Margaret Frohlich for the Anthroposophic Press)

She stared wildly from woods

For this is what is at stake today

I have no photograph of her holding these books

Who sold cancer was selling
cancer?

That was the deed and the nature of polarity

The barn's mind contains everything
from stuffed birds to windsocks

One often gets the impression that
what is emerging now are dark
counter images of light-filled forms
which had formerly pointed to the future

What do we do wounded wastes

Nothing to profess profession

A cloud a house a leaf formed thinking

Sat in the apophatic light thinking naught

Some invisible effigy of books

Autumn and they were cottonwood falls

Winter and December comes down lakes

Thin body frozen at the lacework cuff

Birds entered unbidden hum her hair

Forsaken and dreaming to await winds

Up from a book I open to the first page

A flame from the word *art* projecting

Consciousness and leaves one a one tethered

Stoop to pick up the book after the fire

A hill that does not exist formed suddenly

Antediluvian and the strength of many thousands

Gail Tulloch June 88 inscribed by flyleaf's ghost

It's okay that silence it's okay that it is

ON THE MATERIAL

1.

So the book
comes out of
the woodwork all
voices of theory
torn precepts the
doxa of anti
intellectual quirks

The poet calls
the minute you
pick up her book
red phone in her
bat cave blinking
alert or you
find the map
on which the authors'
names appear in
their actual locations

Though long dead
they reach you
with lines more
material than you
could have imagined
stays and spars
holding your vessel
in place

2.

Hello body of books
flesh of texts
cast about this
yard of fire
what matters
takes up space
quarks and leptons
wave and particle

Made of
what are
made of
time and propinquity
mind over
is the rub

So I ask you
sister of ephemera
can I quote this?
You already have
each cell in your body
a bee in its hive

3.

Maybe we sleep
our way out of this world
ferries without passengers
setting off into
darkening waters
night boats to nowhere
everything enfolds

The I goes on speaking
as though the air
between us was
made material
by words fulminating
like radical breezes
rushing through
isolate leaves

The ripening we
have looked for
is the ripening
that comes after—
the great death
(this is Rilke)
each of us
carries inside
is the fruit

NOTES

4 x 4

These poems were mostly written between February and May 2008, while travelling (or in anticipation or the immediate aftermath of travelling), in Vancouver, Victoria, Calgary, Toronto, Buffalo, Portland, Anaheim, and San Diego. They borrow variously (and sometimes liberally) from: John Ashbery, Charles Baudelaire, Walter Benjamin, Ted Berrigan, Joshua Clover, Jeff Derksen, Emily Dickinson, Stacy Doris, Robert Duncan, T. S. Eliot, Laura Elrick, Roger Farr, Ryan Fitzpatrick, Robert Frost, Peter Gizzi, William Godwin, Goethe, Vicente Huidobro, Fredric Jameson, Charles Lucas, Jennifer Moxley, George Oppen (via Ron Silliman), Ezra Pound, REM, Rilke, The Rolling Stones, Juliana Spahr, Phyllis Webb, William Carlos Williams, Rita Wong, and Slavoj Žižek.

Aristaeus Mourning the Loss of His Bees

Opening line (and instigation of the poem) from Andy Weaver.

The History of Plastic

Closing lines adapted from Lissa Wolsak.

Poem Beginning with the Title of a Cy Twombly Painting

Fifty Days at Iliam is actually the title of a ten-painting sequence by Twombly. One other painting's title from the sequence, *Like a Fire that Consumes All Before It*, also finds its way into the poem.

Pollen

Novalis's original title for his philosophical aphorisms.

Variations and Translations from Rilke's *Book of Hours*
These are homophonic translations—the titles from German, but the body of the texts from one English to another.

Never to Be Possible Said or Sung
The title is taken from Whitman's *Memoranda During the War*: "I kept little note-books for impromptu jottings in pencil.... Some were scratch'd down from narratives I heard and itemized while watching, or waiting, or tending somebody [in the hospitals] ... full of associations never to be possible said or sung.... I leave them just as I threw them by after the war, blotch'd here and there with more than one blood-stain, hurriedly written ... the odds and ends of whatever pieces I can now lay hands on."

ACKNOWLEDGEMENTS

Thanks to the editors of journals work here has previously appeared in: *BafterC, The Capilano Review, Damn the Caesars, dANDelion, Interim, Jacket, Peaches and Bats, P-Queue, Room to Move, stonestone,* and *Tinfish*.

"Rain" appeared previously as liner notes to Rita Costanzi's CD *Song of the Stars,* and as part of an essay entitled "On the Material," in *The Heart Does Break* (ed. George Bowering and Jean Baird).

"Poem Beginning with the Title of a Cy Twombly Painting" previously issued as a broadside by No Press.

Special thanks to Andrea Actis, Jason Christie, Hank Lazer, Jordan Scott, and others too numerous to name.